Tell Me about Your Mother

mamam

maica

matka

morsa

A Collection of Stories to Learn From and Be Inspired By

mutter

mati

mamma

motina

mathair

Lisa Rigato

ISBN 978-1-63814-900-2 (Paperback)
ISBN 978-1-63814-901-9 (Hardcover)
ISBN 978-1-63814-902-6 (Digital)

Covenant Books, Inc.
11661 Hwy 707
Murrells Inlet, SC 29576
www.covenantbooks.com

Dedicated to my siblings—Tony, Lori, and Teri. Also, to my brother-in-law, Jeff, who blessed me with my nieces and nephews, some by blood and some by marriage, but all beautiful blessings—my nieces and nephews, Marie, James, Nicholas, Sara, Andrew, Sean, Joseph, Parris, Christopher, Stephen, Johnny, Mary, Remigius, and Colin. My great nieces and great nephews, Dylan, Brennan, Andrew, Ally, Noah, Joseph III, Conner, Augustine, Bennett-Rose, Reese, Brynn, Hunter, Riley, Vallen, Declinn, Evynn, Alexandra, Kavin, Kelby, Kellan, Killian, Kinsley, Bryson, Alexina, and Charlee-Rose.

Acknowledgments

This book would not be possible without the brilliance of Charlotte Sarnacki. She took my conversations and turned them into living and breathing stories. She is a gifted and talented screenwriter and moviemaker, and I am so blessed to have had her assistance and fingerprint in this project. To see more of her work, visit her website Ridehomefilms.com. My PA, Katie, was also an invaluable asset to me during this process. She helped with transcribing my recordings and was also available for any last-minute panic sessions on getting this project complete. You are an amazing friend and assistant. Destiny Eldred who bailed me out with a great job of transcribing my early conversations and for being willing to share her story here on these pages. My husband, Gary, never stopped believing in this project. He told me from day one that this book was the best idea I've ever had. He was patient and supportive over the very lengthy process of taking this from conception to conclusion. Thank you, my love.

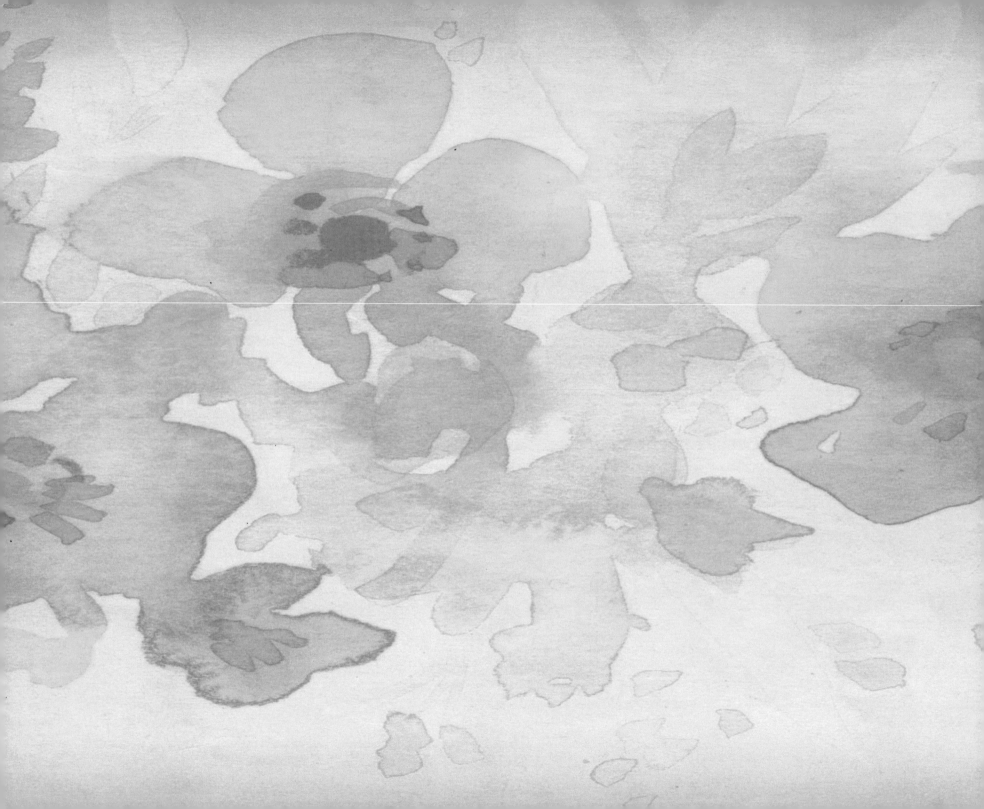

Introduction

For as far back as I can recall, if someone asked me what I wanted to be when I grew up, it was the easiest question to answer. I wanted to be a mom. I remember at an early age, probably eight or nine years old, watching mothers and their children interact. And I imagined what it must be like to have a child that was one-half me and one-half my husband. As I was so young, I deeply romanticized it, and if Pinterest were a thing back then, it would have been Pinterest-worthy! I believed in happily ever after. I married young the first time; it was two months before my twenty-second birthday. I was young, romanticized marriage, and wanted a baby right away. So did my husband. We never used birth control, yet I was unable to get pregnant. Four years into our marriage, I found out he was cheating. I worked very hard to save that marriage, but after another five years of struggling, I divorced him. At that point, I was deeply relieved that I did not have any children with him. I remarried. Too soon and long before the proverbial pendulum had righted itself and I chose poorly. He, however, had a lovely little girl who was six years old at the time and whose mother had died of genetic heart disease. She called me mom, and I was very happy at first. We too decided that we wanted to have a baby and even while undergoing fertility treatments, I could not conceive. After that marriage ended, I was once again grateful that I hadn't had a child with him. During this time of the end of our marriage, he turned his daughter against me, and she believed the ugly lies he told her about me. The good news is a few years after that, she did reach out, and we were able to make peace with one another. Sadly, she ended up dying of the same disease that took her mother at the same age her mother was when she passed away—twenty-seven years old. During all these years of me marrying and divorcing twice and yearning for a child of my own, my sisters and sisters-in-law were pumping out kids left and right. I have two sisters and two brothers and twenty nieces and nephews. I now have a ton of great-nieces and great-nephews. A few years later, after much work on myself and looking inward on what my poor choice in husbands was driven by, I reconnected with a boy from my childhood, Gary Mullins. He truly is the love of my life. When I was forty-two years old, I finally conceived—a miracle! I was ecstatic! I can't really say the same for my poor husband. He was a little shell-shocked. I found out when I was nine weeks along, and I will never forget hearing that heartbeat for the first time or that ultrasound where I swear she waved at us, her little hand moving across the monitor. I was smitten at first glance. When I went to my sixteen-week appointment, they couldn't find a heartbeat. I was devastated. My baby girl had died in the womb, but I hadn't miscarried. I can't really recall the drive home from the doctor's office that day, but my husband came home from work, and my sisters dropped everything and were there by my side. I don't personally have the skill or vocabulary to describe how this felt to me.

Though I have a deep faith, and I trusted that God's plan is always perfect. I did wonder about the why of it—not like "Why me?" but "Why would I have such a strong desire to be a parent yet not be a parent? What am I supposed to do with all this love?" I'm so grateful that I have a lot of faith, and I never doubted the big picture. I knew all of this was part of the life that I had chosen to experience. I know it gave me an enormous amount of empathy for women who experience infertility. I knew with 100 percent certainty that all of this was preparing me for my purpose. And I was determined to use it all for the good of all. As the love of children is at the core of my values, I determined that if I had a child, my focus would've been on that child. But by losing my child, my focus became children. The best way I know of helping children is by helping their parents. It became my desire and purpose to help others achieve their best lives. I became a life coach and believe I am doing that very thing every day. If I can help a person learn to love themselves more, they will be a better parent. If I can help a person learn emotional intelligence, they will be a better parent. If I can help a person make a spiritual connection to the divine, they will be a better parent. If I can help facilitate a tribe of women by giving love and support to each other, they will be better parents. It grew from there. My desire with this book is to share stories of moms and their kids in the hope that a mom who wonders if what she's doing even matters finds inspiration in her mundane daily responsibilities. And if a child was raised by a mom who wasn't present or who was abusive, you will read these stories of triumph and find the inner strength to rise above.

1

Love begins at home, and it's not how much we do...but how much love we put into that action.

—Mother Teresa

Have you ever noticed that when a sports figure is captured on film during a game, how common it is for them to mouth the words "Hi, Mom"? Why? I'll bet that most of them have their fathers to thank as much for the success they have as their mother. I do have a belief about why they do this. I believe it is because mothers are the purest form of love on earth. That is certainly not to say that the love of our fathers isn't a strong and wonderful bond, but the typical role of a father is to teach and discipline and the typical role of a mother is to love and nurture. This is said with the understanding that there are exceptions to every rule. Additionally, there are very successful people out there who have not known the love of a mother or a father. For the sake of argument, let's say that in the average family, the mother loves and nurtures her children within this environment. We flourish and develop into the best versions of ourselves. That is the ideal, isn't it—to be the best possible version of us? I sure do believe that! Come with me on the exploration of individuals and how their mothers influenced them.

Dear Mom...

INSERT PHOTO

2

A mother is she who can take the place of all others but whose place no one can take.

—Cardinal Meymillod

Efren Ramirez, forty-six, is an actor and DJ best known for playing the role of Pedro in the 2004 indie comedy film *Napoleon Dynamite*. He lives in Los Angeles, California. As an actor, Efren Ramirez has always felt that the best way to hone his craft is by connecting with the stories and struggles of others.

Everyone has their own struggles; we all have our road-blocks, and you can't push people beyond their limits. And I am learning, I think, how to not only accept similarities, but to accept differences and go, 'it's okay,' as long as we have that search for the truth.

Perhaps best known for his 2004 film *Napoleon Dynamite*, Efren has had tremendous success as an actor by studying and embracing the lives of others to help prepare him for his roles. Although he has been a working actor for nearly three decades now, he can trace his love for the craft back to his childhood when his mother showed him the importance of perseverance and connecting with others on an emotional level. Efren grew up one of five boys on the east side of Los Angeles, California, the son of Mexican and Salvadoran parents. His father worked as a mechanic at a trucking company, and his mother worked a series of odd jobs, including as a seamstress and as an assistant at the Catholic school Efren and his brothers attended. She could usually be found, however, "maintain[ing] us werewolves and cook[ing] in the house." Efren describes his home life as multicultural, his family embracing their Latin culture and speaking both English and Spanish.

Music was always there, every day. You know, my brothers and I listened to all styles of music and we learned it from our parents. We were able to embrace everything. And it was chaotic. There was a lot of laughter of "boys being boys."

Efren recalls a memorable incident in which as an altar boy, he accidentally got drunk off of wine before a mass one day.

A kid said, "Hey, you can eat the bread; it's not blessed." So, you know, I ate the bread and thought, okay, but because the bread is very dry, there wasn't anything to drink, so we looked at the grape juice and thought we could drink that since it's not blessed. So we were drinking it and drinking it and drinking it. I remember laughing and having such a great time, and thinking, you know, this is going to be awesome! And what I know is that at some point, I was carried to the back of the church, because my brother told me I was laughing really loud and that I was saying, "Jesus is awesome!" My brothers were cracking up going, "Oh my gosh!" So I was no longer an altar boy!"

Music was also a staple of Efren's childhood. When he was twelve years old, his mother helped to convince his father to allow her sons to attend a Depeche Mode concert.

I remember my mom having to say, like, "Okay, if you do good in school, I will get you tickets so you and your friends can go watch Depeche Mode." And we were like, "What?" We were thinking, "Really? Even though they are all goth? Alright!"

Despite the chaos and antics of raising five boys, Efren's mother managed to maintain her household by instilling a strong duty to help others in her sons.

My mother, you learned sense and sensibility. A good sense of who you are, and who you can be. I got that impact from my mother, the "shut up and listen to people and find out what they need, and see if you can provide that." My mom, she really connects to a lot of people, and that is just how she has been since she was little. A funny story—my mother wanted to become a nun when she was younger. And then she met my father, and that changed. Nine months later, that changed. She wanted one of her sons to become a priest, and apparently she wanted me to become a priest, and I had interest in girls, so I was like, "Sorry, not gonna happen!" But I found that my behavior was close to her, and how I am like her. Where sometimes you want to take a back seat really, as if you are aloof in a way so you can really observe what is going on and then you really want to connect mentally and emotionally, and really give and offer something that can move people forward.

Efren's mother taught her kids not only to help others but instilled in them the importance of self-sufficiency and helping themselves. When she wasn't at the school her children attended, she was often at home cooking for her family or taking care of her sons when they were sick, giving her ample opportunity to pass down useful skills and life lessons.

She was always around us. So when we would get in trouble, they wouldn't send us to the principal, they would send us straight to our parents. In the kitchen, she said, "This is my kitchen and as long as you live here, you are gonna learn. I am not here to serve you. You are going to learn how to make ham and eggs, you are going to learn how to make beans and rice, you are going to learn how to make spaghetti."

When Efren's father wasn't working on Sundays, the family would have meals together.

You didn't think about what that habit was going to form until you become the rebel teen, where you're trying to figure things out and your values to anything and everything, and everybody starts to go their own way. So the idea is to hope that both parents kept us together in such a way. My mom sort of taught us how to keep things in the house. Whether we were learning how to cook, or as hard as it was to clean up after ourselves. You know, we were a bunch of guys. It's like my mother having a pack of wolves!

A creative child, Efren recalls spending many of his days playing beneath an avocado tree in his backyard, creating cities and towns with his toys, and receiving encouragement from his mother.

> I would climb the avocado tree and I would just look down at the city I'd created. And then who would find me? My mom. She would go, "Hey, it's time for dinner. What did you create here?"

As he grew older and began to turn his creativity toward acting, he notes that while there were many difficulties along the way, his mother never stopped encouraging him.

> As many times as I was horrible on stage, she would go, "Alright, kid. Mijo, get back up there. Esta bien." Which means "Are you okay?" And I would go, "Si, mama." And she'd say, "Okay. Now get up and do it again!"

It is this perseverance Efren learned from his mother that made him succeed as an actor, eventually leading to his life-changing role of Pedro in *Napoleon Dynamite*, which allowed him to buy a house for his parents. The biggest lesson Efren learned from his mother was that despite any difficulties, you must keep learning, keep doing good for others, and keep moving forward.

> It's that pursuit of discovering new things, and it's not easy, because your heart breaks and breaks and breaks, and you have to learn how to say "It's okay." And I got that from my mom. Do it anyways. Be good, you know. Keep working at it. As an actor, my profession, you live characters' lives, and you really have to go through that fire, and I can do that, but in order to go on a deeper level, you have to look at that through yourself. And I've seen that through my mom, where her heart gets broken but she still does good, and you still have to care for others, and you still have to go, "Hey, it's okay." And you trudge forward slowly and you get up, and you go, "Alright." In the midst of it all, and the pain of it all, you go. And it takes such emotional strength for something like

that. And I get that from my mom. You know, I think somewhere at the end, at the exit, you hear "It's okay. Come on." Or my mother saying "Esta bien. Okay? Vamanos." She said "You okay? Alright. Let's go." And you gotta keep doing it. You gotta forge on.

3

A mother's arms are more
comforting than anyone else's.
—Princess Diana

I remember as a very little girl, perhaps five or six years old, it was a day when I wasn't feeling well. I was home alone without any siblings. As the fourth of five children, this didn't happen very often. I remember my mom coming into my bedroom to check on me and bring me a drink of water, and I asked her to stay with me for a while. Her response was "I don't have time. I have too much to do." As a little girl, that hurt me deeply, and I feel it impacted what and how I asked for things for the remainder of my childhood. This may seem like an extreme reaction, but all I can say is I interpreted that response as "everything else is more important than you." I carried the belief with me for years that my mom didn't really love me. It was last year when I shared that memory with my mom and how it made me feel. She got very emotional and immediately apologized, saying how sometimes moms say things that they have no idea the impact it will have on their children. The apology was healing for me, and I felt instant healing of the hurt I had carried for all those years. It wasn't a big hurt or a daily hurt, but it was there nonetheless, and I am so glad that I brought it up.

Lisa Rigato at four months and her mother, Theresa Rigato

4

Biology is the least of what makes someone a mother.

—Oprah Winfrey

Joseph, his mother and sister Drema are
sitting on the couch from left to right

Joseph Murphy, fifty-four, is a former death-row inmate at the Ohio State Penitentiary. As of September 2011, Joseph's death sentence has been commuted, and he is now serving life without parole. On February 1, 1987, Joseph Murphy, age twenty-one, committed a crime that would forever change the trajectory of his life. Days prior, Joseph's sister, Drema, had been involved in a near-fatal train accident and required a transfer to a larger medical facility in Columbus, Ohio. Lacking the necessary funds, Joseph's brother-in-law, Drema's husband, devised a plan for Joseph to break into the home of seventy-two-year-old widow Ruth Predmore (whom Joseph had done odd jobs for) to acquire objects of value to pay off the family's growing medical bills. On the night in question, Predmore proved to be a bigger obstacle than initially expected, and Joseph brutally took her life, stealing from her a coat, a purse, and a bowl of pennies. The case appeared to be fairly open-and-shut on the surface. Joseph had gotten the idea from his brother, to whom Predmore had been "like a grandmother," to leave a note on her door demanding money; or else he would murder her. Joseph broke into her home and committed the murder when she refused to oblige. At his trial, the jury unanimously recommended that Joseph be sentenced to death. Joseph spent the next twenty-four years of his life on death row, with twenty-three hours a day spent alone in his cell. Though there was no question that Joseph committed the crime, a closer look into his background revealed horrors that eventually led Ohio governor John Kasich to commute the inmate's death sentence to life without parole. Joseph grew up in rural West Virginia. His home was a one-bedroom tar-paper shack for a family of eight with no running water, indoor bathroom, electricity, gas, or phone line where he withstood innumerable acts of neglect and physical, emotional, and sexual abuse. Early on in his life, Joseph's mother and father removed him from school, citing his "hyper" demeanor as the reason, yet refused to get his supposed condition further examined by a medical professional. Instead, Joseph's mother would withhold food from her young son in the hopes that he would lack the energy to require her to be an active parent. Joseph slept tied to the foot of his mother's bed with her forcing him to sleep inside of a trunk. Eventually, Joseph was placed into various homes and institutions by social workers, ultimately having been in seventeen different institutions in four different states by the time he was a teenager. While he was in a home in Pennsylvania, his family moved to Ohio, forcing social workers to track them down to be reunited with Joseph upon his release. A remote child, Joseph argued that his social distance stemmed not from a mental disorder but was merely a defense mechanism. He recalls one nightmarish scenario:

I was just infected. I was sheltering myself from everyone, and liked being isolated. Because when I am around people, bad things happened. One of my younger brothers stabbed me in the head with a knife when I was four years old, and he thought it was funny to see a knife sticking out of my head.

The abuse did not end there. Joseph recalled how, at only five years old, his youth was torn from him when his alcoholic father sold him to be raped by a local moonshine producer to acquire more alcohol. With a mother who "didn't care," Joseph was left to fend almost entirely for himself and to defend himself against his father's endless beatings which, at one point, included being lit on fire. Joseph eventually learned to use arson as a way to distract his parents from abusing him, thus beginning his life of crime. Such unbelievable cruelties at the hands of his parents raise the question of whether or not any person could have survived such a desolate childhood without being susceptible to the influence of others.

> If I wasn't abused or neglected when I was younger, then I would have been able to go to school and take classes like a normal kid, and get an education. And I wouldn't have been easily manipulated or vulnerable to suggestions, and I wouldn't have gotten in trouble by being under the influence of my brother-in-law the night that this happened. I would have just told him, "No, let's ask her for the money instead of rushing in," or I would have thought of something different.

At the bequest of Kathryn Sandford, the defense attorney assigned to him in 1997, Joseph was eventually examined by Dr. Michael Gelbort, a neuropsychologist. Dr. Gelbort determined that Joseph's accounts of his childhood were factual and played a hand in his social development issues. With Dr. Gelbort's assessment, Sandford was able to set a clemency hearing to appeal to state governor Kasich. Kasich overturned Joseph's death sentence, granting him life without parole. Joseph has since been moved off of death row and into the general prison population. Joseph notes that his mother endured physical abuse from her mother, but rather than break the cycle and learn what parenting techniques—or lack thereof—to avoid or change, she became indolent and abusive herself. Although Joseph's father has passed away, his mother is still alive and yet refuses to have any contact with her son.

> She told my attorneys to "go away and don't come no more, because Joey Murphy died a long time ago," and she doesn't want anything to do with anything that concerns Joey Murphy.

Rather than lashing out, Joseph had internalized his mother's abuse and struggles to place blame.

I've always felt it was my fault; that I always did something wrong; that I should have did something different. Everyone still says it's my fault.

While Joseph lacked a proper support system from his immediate family, he had made peace with his situation and had been able to find forgiveness due to his close relationship with God.

I taught myself to read and write, and one of the first places that I ever wrote to was St. Gertrude, the great Roman Catholic Church in Cincinnati, Ohio. And I just asked if they could help me be a better person and be a child of God, because I was thinking of committing suicide because I've never known love in my whole life, and I didn't want to die on death row never knowing. So I was on the verge of committing suicide and just wanted to reach out to anyone who would respond, and Bishop Dolan and his parish responded.

After writing to thirty-one different parishes in the hopes of being welcomed by a religious institute, Joseph had learned true forgiveness and the love that eluded him as a child through the help of St. Gertrude's welcoming bishop and parishioners.

[Love is] not family. I mean, strangers can love you more than your own family can. To me, love is a person that reaches out, and let[s] you know that you exist and what you're doing is important, and that someone loves you, even if you don't know that someone.

And a lot of time the people who do that are religious, and it lets me know that it's Jesus that lives inside of them that lets them reach out to other people. That's the only kind of love I've ever known my entire life. I forgive [my family] and I love them, and I get tearful and choked up when I think of these family members.

To aid in his clemency hearing, Joseph met with his victim's niece, Peg Predmore Kavanagh. Kavanagh acknowledged how the vicious abuse in his early life played a major role in leading to her aunt's murder and agreed that Joseph did not belong on death row. Although love was not ever shown to Joseph by his parents, through the love and forgiveness of others, he had come to learn what properly caring for a child means and had grown from the mistakes made by his parents that were later mended by his supporters.

Love your children while they are children, because they always need to know that you love them. They need to know that you care about them, and always make sure that they know. Hug them and kiss them and tell them frequently that you love them, because when children feel that they are neglected by their mother they tend to fade away into the distance, and no mother needs that or wants that. And they aren't going to stay kids forever. They will grow up to be Christians and who believe in God and know what love is, because love is a very rare thing, and you just need to always let your kids know that no matter what the circumstance or situation is, that you love your children.

5

Motherhood is the greatest thing
and the hardest thing.

—Ricki Lake

Nic Askew is a filmmaker and storyteller best known for his series *Soul Biographies*. Born and raised in London, Nic now resides in the US with his wife, Caroline, and their five children. To learn more about Nic's work, visit Nicaskew.com Although his British boarding school education did provide certain advantages later in life, filmmaker Nic Askew often felt growing up that his natural creative streak and sense of adventure were not being properly nurtured in such a strict, controlled system.

British society, being so structured, doesn't allow for the unusual; the eccentric. I was bored, to be honest. My curiosity wasn't satisfied. I'm pretty sure I lived in my imagination most of the time. I think it was part of the British hierarchical system I was brought up in. A sense of spirit can be stifled in such an environment.

Nic noted that he had a natural flair for the unusual and a sense of curiosity for the world around him—qualities that were not encouraged throughout his educational experience. Despite these set-backs, such an upbringing gave him a sense of what he didn't want for his own life and career as an adult as well as the importance of embracing the unknown.

> I get a sense that this life is not a cut and dry thing, that starts here and ends here, and that's it. The explanation of life…if I'm here, I might as well play with it, in all its beautiful sadness. I'm finding [that] in sharing contributes, I'm pushed into a sense of wonder all the time. I don't necessarily want a set answer. Just always wondering.

Nic grew up the eldest of three boys in a middle-class family, his father a doctor and his mother a nurse. While his home life was also often shaped by rules and regulations

> My mum was structured and organized. She could organize a nation to do something.

It tended to be more relaxed than that of his school.

> To be honest, our conversations were fun, irreverent, British, kind of Monty Python. We joked about death, birth—the most irreverent conversations. Dinners were interrupted because my dad was always on call as a doctor. We had a lot of fun, especially as we got older. We never overtly talked about values. Most values passed on unconsciously.

And although his parents, in the medical field themselves and shaped by the society around them, encouraged him to choose a safe career path, his creative choices were always respected. When he began his profession as a filmmaker, although it seemed an unusual and unsteady occupation, he noted that his mother always supported him.

> In one respect she's always concerned with my career. I remember being a managing director of a company, and it was kind of almost the underlying conversation,

that "I can stop worrying about Nic now." Then, it came down to making these films. There was no struggle with the way it is. I often thought I could really be angry that there were expectations, but in another respect, it was freeing. They didn't get in the way of my choices. Some parents live vicariously through their children, which is a terrible thing. We were left free.

Embracing this sense of freedom led Nic and each of his siblings on many world travels and adventures—opportunities supported by his parents.

We all traveled. I was in the Sahara at a young age, at a time when that just didn't happen. It was my idea, but my [parents] encouraged it too. There was no holding back. At one time, I was in the Amazon, and another brother was in Columbia somewhere, and another brother was in the civil war in Serbia. They had good reasons to worry, but didn't say "We don't want you to do that."

The autonomy and sense of independence instilled in Nic by his parents could not be quelled by his school experience or by societal pressure, which tended to push him toward a more straightforward career. Though he never intentionally set out to become a filmmaker, after a trial and error process of different career paths, he was finally able to land on something that stuck.

I was an explorer. I was seventeen when I crossed the Sahara Desert in a geographical exploration. The decision to be a managing director for a company, I listened to everybody's decisions. Backed out in six months. Then, I made the same decision again; resigned the third day. There's a reason I've made these decisions, despite my better judgment, that got me thinking, "Why?" Assumptions of right and wrong. What people seem to want is to get more and become more, but I get that that wasn't the point of my life.

Nic's adventurous nature and determination to live his life on his own terms had led to an outlook well-suited to his career as a filmmaker and an ability to see life through a variety of lenses. He noted rather than being dissuaded by early formative experiences, he'd been propelled forward by them and found lessons in these struggles. After her own mother died giving birth to her in 1939, Nic's mother was raised with a "cool" upbringing by her grandmother. And while this early trauma was initially painful for her, Nic maintained that it was the very often the difficult parts of life that offered the best growth opportunities—an ideology learned through his own family dynamics:

Jackie Askew with son, Nic

Families have the capacities to propel you into something mystical. When you look at a harsh experience, the world would say, "How awful; that shouldn't have happened." What if it was purposeful in some way? What if it gave way to a lot of pain being overcome?

The freedom to be oneself within a strict and formidable society is a lesson that Nic had passed on, perhaps unconsciously, from his mother to his own children.

We took our daughter to a ballet class. This nation is obsessed with resumes and careers. It was just awful. We found a class that really brought her to life. To do ballet is not enough. To do ballet with joy is perfect.

6

All that I am or ever hope to be,
I owe to my angel mother.

—Abraham Lincoln

Mike Dooley, his daughter Rebecca, and wife Marisol

Mike Dooley founded a philosophical Adventurers Club on the Internet that is now home to nearly one million members from over 185 countries. His inspirational books emphasizing spiritual accountability have been published in twenty-five languages, and he was one of the featured teachers in the international phenomenon, The Secret. Today Mike is perhaps best known for his free *Notes from the Universe* e-mailings and is a best-selling author. Mike lives what he teaches, traveling internationally, speaking on life, dreams, and happiness. Find out more at Tut.com. Born in Great Britain, Mike Dooley's mother, Sheelagh Mawe, imparted in her children from early on the importance of setting one's mind on a goal and taking the necessary means to achieve it. Working several odd jobs throughout Paris and raising her children in Hawaii, New Jersey, and St. Petersburg, Florida. Sheelagh struggled to find her niche in the workforce. Following a divorce, Mike's mother was faced with the additional struggle of maintaining a balanced home life for her children while simultaneously finding work.

She was just kind of petrified and extremely serious about running a household—which she had never done alone before—on a much, much-reduced budget. We literally saved bathwater to water patches of grass in the sun, which we'd sneak around and do. Hopefully, no neighbors saw and wondered what sort of craziness we were up to. She was very strict, a kind of stern taskmaster.

Despite the difficulty of raising her children as a single parent, Sheelagh still managed to follow through with one of her greatest ambitions—becoming a published author.

One of her lifelong dreams was to be a writer, but she never finished the equivalent of high school and really thought that she's no one to dare to have such a dream. But she finally did write Dandelion, the first draft of which was written when she finally settled down into a clerical job. The dedication and the perseverance was unbelievable, because she ran a tight ship and cleaned religiously. In her spare time, she wrote this book.

Mike noted that the success of the novel *Dandelion: The Extraordinary Life of a Misfit* helped Sheelagh to feel more financially secure, and her determination in seeing it succeed was a result of her financial worries rather than a love of writing. Witnessing his mother's willpower firsthand taught Mike and his siblings the value of not simply dreaming but having the perseverance to realize those dreams.

The relationship and upbringing I've had, as directed by my mother, was crucial. She was stern and strict and didn't mind screaming and yelling, which we always hated. She was very, very strong, as was evidenced by her almost selflessness putting together a family, cooking, cleaning, writing, or at a job. A huge amount of discipline was instilled in me. She instilled in me anything and everything is possible. I've always had huge dreams, as had she. I had dreams, even as a kid, for a new bike, a new stereo. Mom would say, "Go do something about it!" Now a published author himself, Mike has taken his mother's advice and turned it into a life as an entrepreneur and philosophical teacher. Leaving a six-figure job as a tax consultant at only 28 years old, Mike attributes that life-changing decision to the values instilled in him growing up, as well as his own path of spiritual self-discovery. When we discovered the metaphysical principles of life—all of us, my brother and sister included—became dreamers. Life isn't about tests and judgments, but about discovering who you are and following your heart. The truth always makes you more spiritual. We're all parts of God, if you will. We all just stopped going to church. We had a bit of hesitancy, but that went away quickly. With all due respect to churches, we found an alternate road map that was more loving, welcoming, and cohesive. We were more inspired to live upright lives. We lost our religion and discovered ourselves, the magnificent spiritual beings we are.

Living comfortably in Florida, Sheelagh had watched her children grow in success in large part due to the ambition and discipline she instilled in them. Learning the value of discovering one's self and intuiting what is right as an individual had been crucial to Mike's sense of self and blossoming career. Yet despite his success, he remained faithful to his roots.

I don't call [my mom] to see what I should do, but I call her as a friend, a compatriot, a fellow life adventurer. To me, home is mom. Wherever mom is, is home.

Mike's mom had passed away since the time of this interview.

Mike Dooley and his mother Sheelagh Mawe

7

A mother is not someone to lean on, but
a person to make leaning unnecessary.
                                —Dorothy Fisher

Erika Deaton-Mohney is a point of care coordinator for Bronson Hospital. A medical laboratory scientist for twenty-five years, she is also a mother to two sons and family to three stepchildren. Erika grew up knowing that despite any setbacks she might face, she had to keep moving forward. This was a lesson instilled in her largely by her mother, Gisela, who saw her own life begin to change as she and her husband divorced in 1975, four years after Erika's birth. While her father eventually married his girlfriend and she became a stepmother and stable presence in Erika's life, Erika credits her mother with holding her family together and teaching her how to move on from this obstacle.

> I grew up knowing both of my parents loved me. I never felt like one of my parents didn't love me. I never felt like I was abandoned. My mom was the one who raised me. Daddy was a really good cheerleader, but Mom was the one who shaped me into who I am.

Erika believes that her mother's strength stems from her childhood growing up in a rural town in war-torn Germany in the early 1940s. Initially born into a wealthy family who owned a car dealership and auto repair shop, the war quickly changed their fortune. Born in 1941, Gisela relayed to her children stories of airplanes flying overhead and fleeing to nearby woods out of fear of her town being bombed. In one incident, when she was only five years old, a German soldier threatened to kill her and her fellow townspeople as they hid out in a local chapel if there were found to be any American soldiers in their midst. Although they survived, it was a traumatizing event. Eventually, her father was temporarily detained, but once released, he demonstrated a steadfast approach to his parenting that Erika believes has been passed down through generations. Her father had moved to the city to rebuild a car repair place so he could move his family there, and then they could survive again.

Erika and her mother, Gisela Walch.

     He showed up at her First Communion. He had taken the train and was very well dressed, and he went to her First Communion. Then, he didn't have enough money to make it home, so she finds out later that he had just enough money to take the train to the next stop, and after everything was done, he got on the train to go home. They all said goodbye. He took the train to the next stop and got off and walked two days home. So that is the kind of parenting I come from.

Although Erika's grandfather died before she was born, she noted that her grandparents "parented fiercely" as did her own mother to her. When her mother was twenty years old, she met Erika's father, an American GI named Wayne. Six months later, despite a language barrier, he proposed to her.

> She was terrified, because she just didn't know. She knew she loved him, but when they first met, she didn't speak English and he did not speak German, and they dated with a little German-American dictionary to communicate. So they got married, and I know that Mom was kind of funny about being terrified, so she kind of dragged her feet, but Daddy was not having it. He brought her to the states and she did not know a word of English.

Four years later, while still learning a new language, her mother gave birth to Erika's older sister, Heidi. Although the early years of their marriage were happy, by the early 1970s things began to change in their relationship, and they eventually divorced in 1975, creating an added layer of loneliness for her mother. Erika notes that all of Gisela's family remained in Germany, her only relatives in the United States being her own children. Despite this upheaval in her life, she continued to be a present and nurturing parent to her daughters.

> She couldn't do the "mom club" things that I would do for the boys, because she worked until 6:00 every night. And Heidi and I had chores we had to do when we got home from school. Heidi had to do dinner and I had to do the dishes, and everything was picked up when Mom came home. We all sat down at the table and had dinner, which I still do to this day with my kids. We have dinner every Sunday.

When Erika was in high school, her mother met Heidi and Erika's eventual stepfather, Dale. Although the pair dated for several years, they waited to get married until after Erika had graduated high school, her mother wanting to wait "until [I was] on my own two feet." Although each of her parents had found new partners, their parenting styles remained very much united.

> I know that growing up, Heidi and I both felt very much that while our parents weren't married, they parented us as a united front. So you couldn't get away with

crap with either one of them. It never even occurred to me that you would play one parent against the other, cause that wasn't going to work. I think they led by example there.

Erika had to learn from her parents how to pick herself up and continue to be a strong mother when her own marriage began to fall apart. After meeting her first husband, Mike, while interning before taking her medical laboratory science board exam, she soon became pregnant with their first son, Michael.

He loved me in the way I needed to be loved, and the way I wanted to be loved. And you have to also under-stand that I have never not felt loved. I always felt loved. And so I wasn't looking for something to replace or make up. I honestly loved this guy. I was head over heels for him.

Four years later, they had their second son, Peter, at which point things began to take a turn for the worse in their relationship. When Michael was five and Peter was only one, Mike left his family.

I had some wonderful years with him. I really did. He was such a good dad.

Michael & Peter Deaton in 2005

Nobody saw this coming. He was amazing. And then he started his way into partying with some people that were into drugs, and I was just not. I am not into it. I don't want it in my house. I don't want to be around it. I don't want to participate in it. I started seeing some drug paraphernalia that was initially just pot. But then it got worse. And then 9/11 happened. That next week I came home and he walked out the door. He put his wedding ring in a little envelope with a "Dear Jane" letter in it and walked out the door. And when he left me and Michael and Peter, he walked out on his mom, his sisters, his brother, his dad, his aunts and uncles. Nobody heard from him. He just went underground.

Although faced with massive disruption to the life she had built, Erika put the lessons instilled in her by her mother to good use and continued to be a supportive parent to her young sons.

Erika & her son
Michael Deaton

Erika & her son
Peter Deaton

I've always had this thing where like, you just pull yourself up and you're not gonna wallow in pain. You put one foot in front of the other, and you can do this. It wasn't even like, "figure your shit out," it was like, you can do this. And I might have had a hot second where I was scared. Who wouldn't be? I had a mortgage, I had a car payment, I had two kids in daycare. And it was just me. And he was gone.

Faced with the sudden difficulties of being a single mother, Erika ensured that despite the loss of their father in their lives, her sons would have everything they needed, being for them a Cub Scout den mother, youth group leader, preschool lunch mom, and wrestling mom all while working full time in a medical laboratory.

That always weighed heavy on my heart. I always wanted to do everything I could to make sure that they turned out okay. I never said anything bad to them about their dad, even though I had plenty to say, and said it very loudly in my own head. I never uttered a word of that, because I knew from my own experiences, you figure stuff out as an adult.

After years of adjusting to life as a single parent, Erika began to date and eventually, after three years of dating, became remarried to her husband Wayne, who has since adopted her sons.

He definitely puts everybody in front of him. Sometimes to the point where I'm like, "Can you put yourself first please?" I have seen him parent Michael and Peter in a way that I know it comes from love. And I know that we grew into that. It wasn't without hiccups when we first moved in together. We first got married and we have five kids in the house, two bathrooms, and only so many candy bars—stupid stuff. It worked because we both honestly wanted it to work. To put everything in front of us to make it work.

Once her sons entered high school, Erika began to build on her career, and she is now a point of care coordinator.

I worked in the laboratory doing testing on humans for 20 years, and then I decided I wanted to change my career. Now, the reason I waited 20 years is because I had little ones. [Now] I do a lot of training for some of the higher, harder tests. I work with a lot of nurses, doctors, MAs, phlebotomists; I work with the CEO of Bronson. I am everybody's gal. I love it.

The difficulties she has faced in her own past have only been surmounted through the determination and tenacity instilled in her by her mother—lessons that began early in Erika's adolescence and continued in their relevance throughout each new chapter in her life.

Mom would tell us to pick ourselves up by our bootstraps. She was just a really big cheerleader. I never thought that there was a ceiling for me. I never thought there were limitations. I went to college right out of high school because I didn't think I couldn't. I moved out and went to college and got my degree in four years. I worked a full-time and a part-time job while I went to college. I graduated with a great GPA and Dean's list some of those semesters.

In addition to demonstrating for Erika the importance of fortitude, she also encouraged in her the benefits of community in coping. Raised in the Catholic Church, Erika remembered her mother's love for singing in the church choir, music being another outlet for her emotions.

When she was sad, she sang. It made her feel better. When there were sad times, it was okay to be sad. That was different to her than wallowing in self-pity. But if we were having a hard time, we cried. We cried together. One of the things Mom would do when she got particularly emotional was play music really loudly. And we would dance around the house, and you think about it, it's crazy. I love those songs. So when I clean house now, I play "Fernando" and all of the ABBA songs.

Erika recalled a recent memory in which she played an ABBA song for her mother, hoping it would spark happy memories for her as it did for Erika.

> I said, "Alexa, play 'Fernando.'" And it started playing and my mom started crying. I felt horrible!

Erika quickly explained to her mother that although the song was painful for her, to Erika it was a joyful memory between mother and daughter.

> I had to explain to her that she had turned the negative, once again, into something that could be looked at as beautiful.

Although once a single mother and forced to navigate the world independently, she noted that she was never truly alone.

Erica Deaton-Mohney and her mother, Gisela Walsh.

> When you play an instrument, you have chair competitions, and if I didn't get it, or if I applied for a job and I didn't get it, she would get right into the gutter with me

43

and pull me out, and she would say "You better pick yourself up by your bootstraps, because you're gonna do it and we're gonna do it and it will work out." She completely cheered me.

Though she had faced setbacks in her life, Erika had never failed to bounce back—a resiliency she believed had been passed down from generation to generation.

I grew up kind of always knowing that if I wanted something bad enough, all I had to do was try. I didn't know there was such a thing as a ceiling. I had no idea.

8

Here's to strong women. May we know them.
May we raise them. May we be them.

—Unknown

Erik Salitan runs the Bushwhack Alaska Guiding & Outfitting Lodge in Wiseman, Alaska, and the Talarik Creek Lodge in Iliamna with his wife, Martha. He is perhaps best known for his role demonstrating survival in Alaska on the National Geographic Channel show *Life Below Zero*. To learn more, visit Bushwhackalaska.com Throughout his time in high school, Erik Salitan found himself faced with prospects for post-graduation life that left him disheartened—the military, a family, paying his own way through college, menial labor, or "get[ting] in trouble with the law. That of course was the most popular choice where I grew up." Although the Finger Lakes area of Upstate New York provided Erik with plenty of chances to explore the local nature through his teenage jobs of lifty at a ski resort, tree topping, hunting, fishing, and working in the woods, opportunities for personal growth were few.

Upstate New York, as nice of an area as it is in many ways, it is the quintessential failure of the "American Dream" and the American economy. There's very, very little opportunity for young people to do anything, if that's where you're from.

For Erik, staying in the Finger Lakes would have been detrimental to achieving any real-life goals partially due to his less-than-perfect reputation.

> I was a bad kid. I got in a lot of trouble. I would have consecutive in-school suspensions for weeks on end. I would even get in some minor scrapes with the law. My name was known by the game warden in Upstate New York.

The quiet rural area gave Erik the freedom to get into trouble, and while it nurtured his love of the outdoors, it left him feeling restless. Erik left home at the age of fifteen, working at various jobs to pay his own rent, utilities, and bills. This independent lifestyle with no real structure or chance for upward mobility led to Erik making "bad choices," but it also helped force him to begin focusing on improvement.

> I was...running around with people who didn't make good choices, drinking beers, but at the same time, I always took responsibility for my own actions, and I always had my mind and my eyes forward.

With his hometown in financial disarray, his peers in legal trouble, and his prospects up in the air, Erik decided to make a future out of the place in which he had been most passionate: the wilderness. Having been an avid outdoor sportsman all his life, Erik decided to embark on a new challenge that would still allow him to spend time connecting with nature.

> I decided I was going to do something different. Alaska hit my radar—just like it says on the license plate, "It's the last frontier"—so the idea of less constraints and social norms, less rules and regulations.

Leaving for Alaska on the day of his high school graduation in 2002, Erik immediately began adopting the go-forth attitude that he sought in his new home.

I got in my 1995, four-cylinder old pickup and drove. That was not an accident. It was about 4,500 miles. People thought I was crazy as shit to do that. I might have been. I had no idea how much fuel would cost. I was operating on a pretty tight budget. I had some nominal possessions for the trip—old shotguns, a rifle. I saved some guns, sleeping bags, and fishing poles for Alaska. I drove up there, and it was an incredible experience, seeing grizzly bears, elk, and caribou. I was like a kid in a candy store. I couldn't believe I made it to this "Serengeti of the North"—this incredible landscape with mountains.

Once he reached Alaska and was able to absorb its natural beauty, it soon became

Erik Salitan & his wife Martha

clear to Erik that contrary to his former home, opportunities for a nature enthusiast such as himself were plentiful here. With the establishment of two successful businesses and the beginning of a family, it became clear that Erik had made the right choice and discovered where he belonged. He began the Bushwhack Alaska Guiding & Outfitting Lodge with his wife, Martha, a native Alaskan; and together they purchased the Talarik Creek Lodge, formerly owned by Martha's father. Both lodges serve as facilities for locals and tourists alike to participate in hunting, fishing, ecotourism, bear-viewing, and photography—all overseen by the couple.

In Bushwhack, Alaska, and the lodge in Wiseman, people laughed when I bought the land. [They said] that I wouldn't be able to build there, or get a road to it. Today, you can taxi an airplane up the house or a 40×40 hangar any day of the year.

While his businesses are thriving, Erik's personal life is also a much happier one than any future he could have foreseen in his hometown.

I currently reside in Alaska year-round. I make my home in Wiseman,

Alaska, which is one of the most northern places in Alaska. It's on the south base of the Brooks Range. We're in the trees, but we're not far from where the trees end and the tundra begins. And it goes up to the north slope, where there are some Eskimo villages. We have the most northern lodge and the most northern hangar in Alaska.

Erik acknowledges that the state has its own issues reminiscent of the problems of the Finger Lakes.

My parents were always very loving. My wife and I are horrified all the time. There are such social problems in Alaska: violence, sexual abuse, alcoholism. Even worse than that, there's just a dip. We try really hard for our little guy. We won't go down that road.

Erik acknowledged the roles that his parents played in shaping both his views on parenting and his own goals in life. Having come from a loving and supportive home where working hard for one's self reigned, he had been able to put such values into action.

Erik Salitan's son Lucas Salitan

50

An incredibly important aspect of my life was my father. If I had asked my father for $1 for a cup of coffee, he would tell me to look in my own pocket. He would laugh in my face if I asked him for anything. Then he would tell me he looked forward to hearing the story of how I came up with it on my own.

Having divorced when Erik was around ten, Erik's time was split between his parents, although not evenly. He noted that having spent more time with his father in his youth, he tends to mirror more of his behaviors than those of his mother's.

My mother was from a different time. My mother is elegant, mentally beautiful, proper and innocent, even in her late 60s. People jokingly used to refer to her as Jackie O because she was so loved, so elegant and kind. My father would say things how they were. He was crude, rude, and honest. I very much ascribed to that ideology much more than my mother's. My mother is such a kind woman. She found a way to get educated, even though it wasn't within the means of her family. She has a Master's degree, on scholarship, in English. If you have a beer with me, I want to talk about the outdoors or business. She's into Shakespearean Lit. I don't relate to her. We don't have a lot in common.

Jacqueline Roberts was born in Upstate New York to a middle-class family where she led an "unassuming" life as a schoolteacher. Erik, being her only child, noted that she was often "left to her own devices" following his parents' divorce.

My mother and father were alienated from each other for a long time. They were both very good to me, although my father was incredibly hard on me. I was always Daddy's boy even when my parents were together. I followed my father like he was Jesus Christ.

Despite their disconnection, one interest the family shared that followed Erik into his adult life was a love for the outdoors and athletics.

When I was very young, I always had an interest in the outdoors. My mother always had an interest in nature also. I started fashioning my own bow and arrows and chasing squirrels around. My father hunted when he was younger, [but] he most certainly wasn't a passionate hunter. He'd done it as something to try with friends. They were very open-minded people. Even though they weren't hunters, they encouraged me to hunt.

Regardless of their dissimilar interests in other areas of life, Erik noted that Jacqueline attempted to play an active role in her son's life.

My mother was a very athletic woman. My mother and I would ski together, both downhill and cross-country. It started where I would ski between her legs. It wasn't long before I'd leave her in the dirt.

Despite its significance, athletics wasn't the only thing Jacqueline instilled in her son that had stayed with him for life.

As much as I am my father's boy, I really should credit my mother that I am a health food fanatic.

Cooking dinner and eating meals together was an important part of family life to his mother, imparting to Erik the importance of clean eating.

My mother would cook healthy food. There was never any junk in our house. 'Til this day I've never had a Coca-Cola, and it's a rarity that I'll eat a bag of chips or something like that. All through 250-plus meals a year, we use organic meat. Meat that we got from the land that is the healthiest.

Eating healthy is integral to Erik's lifestyle, as much of his job requires that he be fit, active, and energetic. Erik credited Jacqueline's dedication to cooking organic and natural foods for her family by encouraging her son to do the same into his adulthood. Erik's unconventional way of life has left him physically unable to connect to his family, and he noted that communication with his mother was limited. However, he speaks to his step-mother daily or bidaily, and he has formed a tight-knit relationship with his half-sisters as well. "It's difficult to relate to my mom in many ways," Erik admitted, relating to the fact that he had inherited more personality traits from his father than his mother. Although his current state of being bares little direct correlation to Jacqueline's influence, Erik remains grateful to both of his parents for allowing him the freedom to follow his exceptional path. From struggling to find his niche in his hometown to thriving in "the last frontier." Erik's experience has been largely rewarding and, thanks to the loving yet relaxed nature of his parents, uniquely his.

Eric Salitan, his wife, Martha, and son, Lucas.

9

A Real Mom: Emotional, yet the rock. Tired, but keeps going. Worried, but full of hope. Impatient, yet patient. Overwhelmed, but never quits. Amazing, even though doubted. Wonderful, even in the chaos. Life changer, every single day.

—Rachel Martin

Destiny Eldred is a forty-year-old stay home mother of two (who feels like a taxi driver) and volunteers at the school, church, and the local humane society. Destiny and her family are living in Port Huron, Michigan. Growing up in the small town of Mayville, Michigan, with her mother, Becky, and younger sister, Lacey, Destiny Eldred learned early on that unlike the parents of her classmates, her mother's struggles with being a single parent and the ensuing emotional damage she experienced left her unable to properly care for her daughters.

Part of [it] was due to my mom's young age. Plus, she was in and out of relationships. She yelled and hit to get her point across to us. She was emotionally absent to me because of her age; she was preoccupied with herself and with trying to get and keep a man.

Destiny and her sister relied on the support of Becky's parents as a "stabilizing force" in their lives and relied on welfare for financial support as their own mother was overwhelmed with putting herself through college, maintaining jobs at a form-manufacturing plant and as a clerk and juggling personal relationships, all without the assistance of either Destiny's or Lacey's father. Despite acknowledging that Becky "has an awesome work ethic and is a perfectionist," she did not properly provide for Destiny's emotional and mental health; and when she became a sophomore at her Christian high school, the tension at home increased to the point where Destiny no longer felt safe.

I decided to confide in my principal, who went to my grandma's church, that the tension and abuse at home had been escalating, and I had the marks to prove it. So of course, she had to report it. Being divorced and living apart and away from my school in North Branch, Michigan, my grandparents were in no position to take me. My principal, a 60-ish aged woman, had had foster girls before, so she was allowed to take me.

Despite the rocky adolescence due to her strained relationship with her biological mother, Destiny, through her strong born-again-Christian beliefs, had managed to build a safe, nurturing, and loving home for her family—her husband of seventeen years, Trevor, and children Andrea (twelve) and Joshua (eight).

Becoming a born-again Christian at 14 changed the trajectory of my life. I began befriending positive friends who were making positive choices. I began studying hard to get good grades, and trying to make a positive future for myself.

After graduating high school, Destiny went on to study visual arts at Spring Arbor University and credited her secure life as a wife, teacher, and mother to her close relationship with God. Yet Destiny admitted that she did not transition from her unstable youth completely unscathed.

I have been dealing with a medical diagnosis of depression for years. I'm on top of it with the help of medication and counseling. It can be exhausting and make life harder than it is for the average person, but it has taught me so much about simplifying and depending on God. It has also taught me grace and forgiveness and has allowed me to let go of the tough stuff with my mom from childhood.

Because of her deep religious beliefs, Destiny had learned to utilize her struggles with depression to create a closer relationship with God as well as with her family.

When I surrendered my life to the Lord Jesus, I learned that nothing in life is more important or valuable or worthwhile than seeking after Him and knowing Him. To me, that is success. Throughout my twenties, I struggled with life's unfairness, and it made me bitter instead of better. [God] answered our prayers and we're more blessed today than we ever dreamed.

Trevor and Destiny Eldred with their kids Andrea and Joshua.

As for her parenting style, Destiny has forged her own path to being a successful mother.

I learned more what not to do than what to do while raising kids from my mom. She didn't take us to church, have regular meals at the table with us, pray with us, etcetera—all the things that are important to me, and for me, to do.

From depending on her grandparents for stability to eventually living with a foster mother, Destiny was able to create her own happy ending despite the roadblocks that threatened to stand in her way, noting that through her beliefs, acceptance had been found.

Through my own struggles and hang-ups, brought out by being a mom, I've accepted the truth that the abuse, the not knowing my father, the other "disadvantages" and "struggles" were nothing to take personally. I used to take it as a reflection of me somehow. Now I know that life can just be hard. People have problems. Hurting people hurt people. But I've grown to find acceptance, grace toward myself and others, and hope. Some wonderful things come with age!

10

What can you do to promote world
peace? Go home and love your family.
—Mother Teresa

Brad Zimmerman, a sixty-six-year-old actor, has written a hilarious and inspiring story about the grit and passion required to "make it' as an artist and the sweet rewards that come from never giving up on your dream. Brad moved to New York City and "temporarily" waited tables for twenty-nine years while continuing to pursue his dream of comedic acting. He never gave up; and many years later, he's opened for Joan Rivers, Brad Garrett, and the famed George Carlin. Brad now has his own touring show, *My Son the Waiter, A Jewish Tragedy*, that is as profound as it is entertaining.

At eighty-nine years old, Barbara Zimmerman has always been a hard worker. Growing up in Sunnyside, Queens, and the Lower East Side, she instilled in her three sons a strong work ethic by working three jobs at once—as a decorator, assisting her husband with his trade, and at a drapery business in New Jersey. Her eldest son, Brad, attributed his sense of determination to his "businesslike" mother yet acknowledged that his uncertain career path gave her pause at first.

> At one time, she believed that I would never make it. She wanted me to work for my father, but she didn't pressure me to do it. She knew, ultimately, that I would follow my own path.

After years of waiting tables, Brad had followed his own path, writing a one-man show and performing his stories professionally for over a decade. The creativity Brad had displayed throughout his life was also partially credited to his mother, a "vibrant, very popular, very beautiful" woman. Barbara pursued an acting career early on in her life.

She studied acting, and they told her she didn't have that much talent, which wasn't necessarily true. She bought into it, so she went for mainstream America.

Although Brad admitted that his mother enjoyed her upper-middle-class lifestyle full of "jewelry and great clothing and great food and parties," he affirmed that personally choosing a more unconventional career path had been essential to maintaining his sense of self.

I got some of my mother's creativity and work ethic. There wasn't a lot of discipline, so therefore all of the stuff I have now—the 'workaholic,' the focus, the discipline, the intensity, the goals—I think a lot of it comes from me. My inner makeup is somebody who needs to be performing in front of other people and being creative. So I think I got a little bit of it from my mother, but most of

Barbara Zimmerman and Brad, at his bar mitzvah along with his brothers and father.

it from me. I attribute it to my own sense of what I'm about.

Brad admitted that his mother's idea of success was typically derived from income, a quality based on her own experience growing up poor. However, Brad noted that in doing what he loved, "she does definitely consider me successful." Although the purpose of Brad's career had never been fame, he had mastered his craft and found a way to "bring joy to people, to entertain, to lighten people's loads and to inspire people"—a gift his mother finds had led to a unique sense of success. Brad's family had its roots in working hard, a trait that has been passed on from mother to son. Yet he had broken with the traditional American family mold set forth by his parents, forming a fulfilling career that had spanned the nation sharing the stories of what he has learned. Although Brad's path strayed from that of his mother's and his identity has been formed through much of his own experience, he noted that no matter his career, when it comes to his mother, "You could always feel the love."

11

Life doesn't come with a manual,
it comes with a mother.

—Unknown

Kim Holstein, along with her husband, Scott, is the cofounder of Kim & Scott's Gourmet Pretzels. Their pretzels can be found in supermarkets, movie theaters, schools, restaurants, and more nationwide (Kimandscotts.com). As a native of Houston, Texas, Kim Holstein noticed that many of her childhood memories tended to revolve around food. "A lot of our family memories and fun times centered around holidays and eating. We are a very food-oriented people. It's part of our culture and part of our life; always has been," Kim stated. Growing up with an older brother, younger sister, and entrepreneur father, Kim noted that the more traditional aspects of her childhood—such as her mother preparing dinner for her children—helped shape her outlook on the importance of both meals and family. Now that she had a husband and children of her own, family breakfasts and dinner are a major part of their lives together. However, at around the time when Kim turned thirteen, her mother also began her own linens company, inadvertently becoming a model for the work ethic that has in part led to Kim's success running her own company.

It's really funny because if you had asked me when I looked back on my life, how I could remember growing up, I wasn't necessarily thinking that my parents were influencing my career. But now when I look back on it, both my mom and my dad, who also had his own business and who retired just a few years ago, were entrepreneurs for many years…You know, in retrospect, I think that [my mother] gave me a lot of tools and a lot of great gifts that have helped me to be successful in many ways.

Food and business were two major aspects of Kim's early life, and therefore it may come as no surprise that Kim's career as the founder of a food company has taken off, its success in part due to Kim's passion for what she does. In the early 1990s, following graduate school at Northwestern University in Chicago and while working in advertising, Kim read an article about homemade pretzels that would change the course of her life.

I became obsessed with pretzels, and had an idea to put flavors inside and on top of them to make all these different flavored pretzels.

When Kim met her husband Scott in 1994, he had also heard about "this crazy pretzel idea" and supported Kim's interest. In May 1995, Kim & Scott's Gourmet Pretzels took off, eventually becoming the nationwide company it is today. While there is no doubt of her business's success, some still wondered, "Why pretzels?" Kim explained:

The pretzel was invented in 610 AD by Italian monks as gifts for children after prayer, and so the twist of the pretzel is actually arms folded in prayer. It's a really spiritual and meaningful product, and I believe it carries a lot of magic and inspiration for my life with my kids and with Scott and I in our lives. It's really been a powerful vehicle for that purpose in our lives and our business.

Now that Kim had a family and business of her own, she had taken the life lessons taught to her from her mother to her own children. Following her own path, even if perhaps unconventional or difficult, was exactly what Kim felt her mother would want for her.

My parents have always cheered me on in my dreams and in our business. They have really been fabulous champions and supporters of us and at the end of the day, I think they want us to be happy.

Kim noted that her own experiences in motherhood had helped her find a balance between business, family, and personal fulfillment as well as led to a better understanding of her own mother.

I think that being a mom was a really big turning point, because with that transition I got this incredible understanding of "wow, she went through this." My girls will say something, and I call my mom and remember when this happened with us. It's like universal karma that I can step into her shoes. She really tried so hard, and she really did love me. Maybe I just didn't feel it or feel understood, but really she was just trying her best.

From food to entrepreneurship to family, Kim's successes have been shaped by her mother with her own twist.

12

It's not easy being a mother. If it
were, fathers would do it.
—Dorothy, *The Golden Girls*

Luciano Del Signore, a fifty-five-year-old award-winning chef and restaurateur, is the head chef and owner of Italian restaurants Bacco Ristorante, Bigalora Wood Fired Cucina, and Casa Pernoi located in and around Southeastern Michigan. In 1957, when Luciano's mother, Lina Del Signore was fifteen years old, she married her husband in her native town of Fonte De Amore, Abruzzo, in Italy. Although the marriage began after World War II, the scars of the war remained, and the land that had been decimated remained unusable. Both Lina and her husband came from a family of farmers, and with their corner of Italy having taken a violent blow, the couple decided shortly after their wedding to make the move that many of their peers and contemporaries globally were also making—to the United States. However, in the 1950s, a wife was unable to immigrate to a new country until her husband, journeying alone, could prove that he had obtained a residency for his family. Thus, it wasn't until five years after her husband had been living in America that Lina was able to join him, and ten months after her arrival that they had their first child together followed by a second and third. Luciano Del Signore, the second child born to his parents, recalled the hard work that was the center and lifeline of most of his childhood. Shortly after their move to the United States, Luciano's father opened his first restaurant, an Italian eatery called DiGiovanni's Pizzeria. The restaurant quickly became a family affair with Lina and the children helping to run the business.

> She gave him support, did his books as much as she could, without leaving the house a lot. I remember when we opened the restaurant Fonte d'Amore in 1974, we were not even teens yet. I remember—can't tell you how many nights—we'd go to school, and then to the restaurant, do our homework at the office, then wash dishes or bus tables a few hours. I remember being woken up in a booth and taken home. I was raised in the restaurant. If it was busy or my dad needed help, my mom was willing and the kids were there, too. Once he got enough help, we had more of a home life.

And although the restaurant was a huge success, with enough momentum to eventually open a second and a third, for the Del Signores, work was not limited to the food industry. Lina worked out of her home, doing drapery and seamstress work to stay close to her children. With her family still overseas, Luciano notes that his mother was his primary caretaker; and although his passion for food and cooking was honed at the family restaurants, the discipline was instilled in him by his mother.

> At home, my mom was always cooking; always doing something. In the summer, we'd pick forty bushels of peppers, roast them on the barbeque pit in the backyard, eat them all day long. That was more her, more instrumental in that kind of stuff. All that stuff was done at home, not at the restaurant.

Although his parents established themselves in the United States early on, Luciano recalled that finding a balance between their Italian heritage and their present American lives was important to the family.

It's funny. My dad, in the most broken accent you've heard in your life, would say, 'I'm an American.' He's really proud of his Italian heritage.

It was perhaps this pride that allowed for Luciano and his siblings to travel to Italy as often as they liked to ensure their close family ties.

The kids, we got to go to Italy—me and my brother, one year him, one year me—as much as we wanted. They would never let us go together, because they knew we'd be glued together and speak English. They put us on a plane [and] find someone who was traveling to Italy to keep an eye on us. As soon as we got on the ground, my grandpa would be waiting for me.

Luciano Del Signore and his mother, Lina Del Signore.

Luciano's travels to Italy would not be limited to his childhood, however. After leaving culinary school after only one year at age nineteen, he traveled to Italy and spent about eight months gaining experience that would later prove invaluable and getting to know his family. Upon his return to the United States, Luciano helped his father remodel their second restaurant and open their third before venturing on his own and opening his own restaurants, Bacco Ristorante in 2002 and Bigalora Wood Fired Cucina in 2010. The success he's had at the restaurant business had been in large part due to the sense of discipline that was established in him thanks to his mother. Luciano recalled that although she stayed busy helping to support her husband and working from her home, Lina was able to be active in her children's lives, teaching them everything from the basics of cooking to regularly bringing food to the underprivileged families of their community. Luciano stated that although he had a family and business of his own, Lina continued to be the mother that she had been since his childhood.

> She still calls me, and we don't talk about the weather. It's all about "Why don't you do this [or] do that with your kids?" I'm fifty-five and she's still mothering.

From a young immigrant wife to a stay-at-home mother and worker, Lina has been instrumental in shaping her children's work ethic and family values. However, perhaps the most lasting impression Luciano had of his mother was also the most important: "When I think of my mom, I think of love."

13

Nothing is really lost until your mom can't find it.
—Unknown

Renee Chodkowski is a cooking instructor and the owner of the Great Foodini. Her work has been featured on *Good Morning America*, *MasterChef*, *Jamie Oliver's Food Revolution*, and Fox 2 News Detroit. She currently hosts a radio show, *Foodini Fridays*, on Livingston County's Own 93.5 WHMI (Thegreatfoodini.com). When thinking of her family and growing up in Livingston County, Michigan, one word comes to mind for Renee Chodkowski: *food*.

Every Sunday, we'd get together at one of the grandma's houses for this wonderful food-fest. I have always associated family with food, love, and happiness. It's no surprise I love to cook.

From a young age, Renee understood the significance of family meals and the ability home-cooked meals have to bring people together. Her grandmother owned and operated Lucy & Hazel's 11 Mile Diner in Royal Oak, Michigan, where a young Renee would watch as her mother helped to feed the hungry crowds.

It was so neat because we'd have this influx of people at breakfast and influx of people at lunch. My grandma said, "If you feed them, they will come." And for some reason, those words stuck in my mind.

Renee personally learned the truth in her grandmother's words when, as a school secretary, she began to try her hand at cooking as a mere distraction at first after her children had gone to sleep. Despite her intentions and introverted demeanor, Renee's meals caught the attention of several coworkers, friends, and family; and she found herself "roped" into teaching a cooking class, from where she found her passion, spawning a multitude of classes, TV appearances, and her own radio show.

I actually still am very shy, but if it involves food, I can do it. That's my thing—I can do that... Food's hot right now. I guess I am a big ham. I like to talk to people, make them laugh and have a good time.

While food has always been an important aspect of Renee's family life, her mother, Elizabeth (or Princess Lizzy as the family liked to call her), taught Renee more than how to cook. Renee credits her mother as a guiding force in her life; a compassionate woman with an equal flair for fun and hard work. While her husband worked outside the home, Elizabeth ran a hair salon from their basement while raising (and of course, cooking for) her two children. After Renee's father—the king of the household—passed away, she noted that Elizabeth's strength in providing for her family magnified.

I'm a super hard worker. I know exactly what I want to be successful. My mom's job was to keep food on the table and stuff. After my dad died, she had to support herself. I did learn a lot from her. I saw someone who wasn't afraid of hard work and somebody who could find a way to make things happen. She was very, very selfless.

Renee noted that the loss of her father "broke things up a bit" for their family, changing the dynamic.

Renee and her mother, Lizzy

We lived on a lake. It'd just be the four of us, me, my brother and parents. The four of us were really close. Some of my best memories are the four of us sitting around the table.

And while Renee acknowledged that while there are aspects of her parents' child-rearing that she has chosen to disregard such as the traditional gender and family roles her parents enforced, she had been able to look to her mother as a role model for determination, perseverance, and commitment.

She would speak of the satisfaction of taking the time to do [things] well. If my mom committed to something, she was going to do it well. And that's how I tried to bring my kids up.

Although Elizabeth instilled a sense of fortitude in her daughter, Renee noted that she also taught her the benefits of living in the moment and loving those around her.

Renee discussed her mother's last minutes before she died in which she reached up and called out the names of her late parents, sister, and husband as one of the most rewarding and insightful memories she retains of her mother.

So, this is my gift. I was so happy. My mom was not a religious person; we went to church sporadically. It bothered me a little bit that she didn't go to church, but at that moment, I learned that it just didn't matter. I became a different person at that moment. Prior to that moment, I used to be a "Type A" driven person. After that moment, everything filtered down through that experience.

Renee stated that her philosophy toward parenting and life was now to be present and aware with the children and family in your life, the last gift Elizabeth was able to give to her daughter. Renee's major successes in the food industry were easily credited to both her own hard work, passion for food, and love of family—traits that have been the foundation of her family for as long as she can remember.

Mom insisted—no matter what—on the weekends, we'd all sit down to a family dinner. It didn't necessarily have to be home cooked, but we were going to sit down and talk. Food is love.

14

Great job, Mom. I turned out awesome.

—Every kid

I was raised in a very traditional Catholic household. When I divorced my first husband, I was still "married" to him in the eyes of the church and my parents. When I decided to be in another relationship, my parents disowned me. What that meant is I was not welcome at their home. I was taken out of the will, and they stopped talking to me. This was devastating to me at the time as we used to be a very close family. After a year or so, I began reaching out to my parents with Christmas cards, birthday cards, and eventually phone calls. They softened a bit, but when my dad passed away six years later, we were still on very cool and distant terms. But the day before he had his life-ending heart attack, he called and asked me to pick up something at the store for him as my mom wasn't home at the time.

Little did I know on that day, it would be the last day I would see him alive. Over the years since then, my mom and I have reached an understanding. We respected each other's beliefs and have a relationship that fit within our defining differences. This didn't happen quickly, and it wasn't without tears and resentment. But I understood that though this was not how I would choose to parent, I respected that she had to do what she believed was right for her. I love my mom and am thankful that at eighty-six years young, she is healthy and happy.

Lisa Rigato and her mother, Theresa Rigato.

15

There's no way to be a perfect mother,
but a million ways to be a good one.

—Jill Churchill

Pastor Ben Walls is a retired preacher from the Brighton Nazarene Church in Brighton Michigan with his church averaging 850 attendees each Sunday. He is a husband, father of two, and grandfather to four. Being born to a stay-at-home mother and a coal miner father as the second oldest into a family of sixteen in Southern Indiana, Pastor Ben Walls's mother learned early on a sense of responsibility and integrity. Pastor Ben, as he is fondly referred to, noted:

I always noticed that my grandmother would make sure that my grandfather would have food first. I asked my mom [why]and she said, "Ben that's from a habit. When I was raised with those fourteen other brothers and sisters, if [my father] went down, we were all done for, back in those days. He ate first, and when he was done, we divided up the rest." Women back then didn't work; his was the sole income, and it was pretty meager. I have a picture of my mom when she was probably ten, and it almost makes me cry. She's dressed in this little, poor, looks like a little orphan dress, dirty face. Haircut with a pair of scissors, bobbed off.

When his grandfather started bootlegging to earn extra money for his family, Pastor Ben describes his mother's upbringing as having entered "survival mode." When she was sixteen, his mother married his father, who was twenty-four years old, "which would be scandalous these days. But back then, with a family as large as theirs, it was a relief to have one less mouth in the house, and so it wasn't any big deal." Facing the incredible pain of losing two of their children early on in their marriage, Pastor Ben explained that his mother and father worked tremendously hard to provide for their surviving three children. His father, also a preacher, worked for a small church; thus, his income, totaling roughly $90,000 over his entire thirty-five-year career, was not nearly enough to support his family by itself. Although the church provided utilities and often groceries for the family, Pastor Ben's mother got a job at the Western Electric Company that, with its benefits and additional income that helped the family save, he described as "their salvation." Being born into a religious family, Pastor Ben explained that to his parents, a relationship with God and a strong moral compass were lauded above all else. His earliest memories include being reprimanded for such deviant childhood commonalities as lying and smoking, suggesting that ensuring that their sons were on an ethical path was of the utmost importance. Pastor Ben explained that while his parents "always seemed like they were on the same page" regarding their children and their relationship toward one another lacked any signs of obvious dissent, it also lacked any outward affection.

I cannot picture my mom and dad hugging. I can't picture them fighting. I did always have a sense of commitment and that they loved each other, but there was just never any show of emotion in our house.

Yet despite their lack of emotion toward each other, Pastor Ben noted that his mother always demonstrated affection and love for her children, making sure to tuck them in at night, pray with them, and hug and kiss them. His father, he noted, was not always so affectionate, until one scenario in which his wife stepped in to unite father and son.

Mel, (Ben's wife), knew that I had never hugged my dad, and he was getting older at that point. We were getting ready to leave. We were on the front porch. Mel spoke up and said, "Ben, hug your dad." Well, to my shame, I guess, and to both of us, it was a very embarrassing moment. But I did reach over and hug him— and by the way, he never let me leave again without a hug.

Pastor Ben noted that throughout his youth, he had a very close relationship with his mother, giving both of his parents credit for the upbringing they gave him and his brothers.

My mom didn't even have a high school education. She quit school, married my dad, and never went back to school. My dad had a high school and then college education and became a pastor. But they both lived such a good moral life. They both modeled integrity to the nth degree. When my wife and kids and I went to visit them in Florida, late in their years, I'd left a dollar worth of change. When I got back the next year, she gave it back when I visited. She had that kind of honesty that would almost drive you a little bit nuts, just to give you an idea of the kind of integrity I was raised under. Telling lies or half-truths was death to us. You just didn't do that. I look back on it, and I'm very grateful for the way they raised me.

The strong sense of integrity, truth, and prayer that Pastor Ben's parents instilled in him had allowed him to raise his own children under the same values and thus a belief in God and, in doing what was right, had been passed down from generation to generation thanks to his parents' teachings. And while he did learn from his parents what he wanted to pass on to his children, he also, in some respects, learned how to improve. Pastor Ben imparted his own parenting advice.

You slow life down, say prayers with them, tell them you love them and hug them. My mom did that, but my dad didn't. I worked hard with my son and my daughter to break that chain. When you feel something so deeply, you can forget to say it. It's so easy to correct; it comes out so automatic, trying to parent our kids. When do we say, "You're the greatest thing in all the world to me!"

16

Dear Mom, thank you for keeping
all the bad stuff I did from Dad.

—Unknown

Laura Mullins is the former owner and current senior advisor of Moylan Energy Management (now Genea), a commercial utilities company based out of Canton, Michigan. Moylan Energy has been awarded the Outstanding Service Award two years running by the Metro Detroit Building and Owner's Management Association (BOMA). Laura now resides year-round in Punta Gorda, Florida.

As a businesswoman and entrepreneur, Laura Mullins had always been adept at pursuing her goals with precision and not letting life's obstacles stand in her way.

I consider myself a very strong individual; a very strong woman. Don't tell me I can't do something. I will prove you wrong.

It is this attitude that allowed her to see her business, Moylan

Left to right: Samantha Moylan (Laura's niece), Nancy Moylan (Laura's mother), Olivia Moylan (Laura's niece), and Laura Mullins.

Energy Management, thrive under her direction for over twenty years, becoming a well-known and award-winning energy company in the Metro-Detroit area. Though Laura sold the business in July of 2019, she had stayed on as a senior advisor and looked forward to the next chapter of her life, including spending time with her husband, nieces, and grandchildren.

> I think the next part of my life is going to be more of the defining part of my life, and that kind of scares me. Because it feels like I have responsibility there, but it's going to be a journey in itself.

Laura was born into a large middle-class Irish-Catholic family, a middle child between an older brother and sister and two younger brothers.

> Twenty-five grandchildren for my grandparents on one side, and twenty-six grandchildren on the other. Lots of first cousins and many of them I am very good friends with.

In 1973, when Laura was around twelve years old, her parents started Moylan Energy Associates, Inc., an engineering consulting firm that put them securely in the upper-middle class. While her mother initially worked for the family business, she later became a stay-at-home mom when Laura was a teenager.

> I would come home from high school and I would walk in the door and smell cookies baking, and I was like, oh my God, this is a whole fairytale, Beaver Cleaver-type world. And obviously I didn't know what was going on with them.

Although life seemed happy and stable to Laura and her siblings, beneath the surface her parents faced many marital issues that would eventually lead to their separation and divorce when Laura was in her early twenties.

We weren't big on communication. We weren't necessarily close, and my parents weren't necessarily close. Which is kind of disappointing. It wasn't like an ideal family situation.

Laura partially credits her family's relationship with their Irish Catholic roots for creating distance and guilt amongst themselves.

An Irish Catholic should be like this, you should go to church, etc with lots of conditions on what is right and acceptable. But at the time, it was also a feeling of if something good happens, just wait, because the other shoe is going to drop and it's a balance, because some crap is about to hit you in the face. And to this day, something great is going to happen that is going to become something terrible, and that's not true. It's a little bit of how I was brought up, and it is one of those where you almost have to fight for happiness. And that shouldn't be a fight.

Laura's life changed dramatically when, in her early thirties, she met her husband Larry, her "knight in shining armor." Larry was still grieving the recent loss of his wife, Cindy, who had passed away from leukemia and grappling with the struggles of raising two teenage boys by himself. After their first date, it was Laura's mother who encouraged her to give him a second chance, "which thank God she did, because he is my soulmate." Laura, who had never been married and had no children, was suddenly plunged into the role of a wife and caregiver to teenagers who were still grieving the loss of their mother. While Larry's sons did open their arms and invite Laura into her new role in their family, Laura credited Cindy with helping to smooth the transition.

Cindy put me, I think she selected me—I know she selected me, 100%, she selected me for [Larry] and she selected [Larry] for me, and she selected me for the boys in the way that they needed.

She recalled one particular Christmas Eve shortly after their marriage when the reality of her new life weighed heavily on her. Home alone with her stepsons, things came to a boiling point after an argument.

> I can remember kind of screaming at them and walking into our bedroom and our bathroom and I ran myself a bubble bath, which I normally don't do. And I am soaking in the bubble bath and I can remember thinking and talking to their mom saying, "So help me God, you better get me through this, because I want to kill them!" And I always knew she picked me, but I'm like, "You better get me through this!"

Her marriage to Larry turned out to not only be a major adjustment to her personal life but was a pivotal factor in her career as well. Though Laura may have inherited her business savvy from her father, he was not her biggest supporter. And when it came time to buy Moylan Energy from him in 1999, "he was one I wanted to prove wrong, in a certain sense. You go with your gut. My dad was the one who never would have thought I could do anything right. My mom thought I could walk on the moon. I found myself leaning toward the positive energy of my mother." Despite the lack of support from her father, Larry encouraged her to find the confidence to take over the family business.

> There was a part of me that believed [my father] when he said I couldn't do it, but then I also had my mom say that I could do anything. I don't know about that, but then I had Larry, who said "We can do this." He kind of put it in perspective. What's the worst that could happen? We lose everything and we live in an apartment and we start over. And that was scary for me, but at the same time it was an out for getting out from under my dad, which was more scary than losing everything.

With Larry's support, Laura signed the papers to take over Moylan Energy on their fifth wedding anniversary.

I always joke that for our 5ᵗʰ anniversary, he bought me a company. Which, the 5ᵗʰ anniversary is paper, so technically, it was perfect!

Becoming a business owner didn't always seem possible to Laura, who as a child struggled with dyslexia. She noted that for most of her childhood, she maintained average to below-average grades until high school where she had to work hard to earn above-average grades. Although her dyslexia diagnosis presented issues, Laura recalled that at first, it was a source of jealousy between her and her sister.

> My older sister who is three years older than me was diagnosed with dyslexia, so she would have to go to the doctor and get tested and go to therapy every other week. And of course as your older sister, seeing this, you tend to glorify it, and I thought, "Oh man, she is getting attention from my mom, and she has this one-on-one time with my mom going to these things." So I sort of wanted to be dyslexic. That's why they say be careful what you ask for.

With her mother's encouragement, Laura was able to get through the extra homework, therapy, and doctor's appointments that accompanied her own dyslexia diagnosis.

> Dyslexia obviously is a hindrance. It's an obstacle, but my mom pushed and wasn't going to let that be a factor.

Laura eventually learned to see her dyslexia not only as something that she could overcome but as an asset to use to her advantage.

> Obstacles are only an excuse, which are valid excuses, and I am not judging. It's just a part of who I was. It doesn't define me in any way, shape, or form. Actually, I consider dyslexia an asset in so many ways. The dyslexia has been more of an asset to me in my life than anything other than my mom. I look at it as an advantage, because it teaches

you. From a very young start, you are thrown this obstacle right into your face, and from a very young start you figure out how to get around them. You kind of figure out how to go over it or around it or divert. That's a huge skill in life.

Laura applied these life skills while acquiring her business, never losing her can-do attitude. Her parents both contributed to her success in different ways—her mother having helped her learn to overcome obstacles and her father giving her the determination to prove his doubts wrong.

If somebody tells you you can't climb on top of a mountain just because you didn't think about climbing a mountain, you might look at it and say, "Wanna bet?" And then you might think in your gut, "I'm going to climb that mountain." So climb that mountain! If your gut says "I can do it," do it! Your gut knows more than anybody else knows.

While her mother helped Laura overcome her dyslexia diagnosis and went on to support Laura's transition into a businesswoman, she noted that their relationship was not always smooth, particularly as Laura was growing up.

She didn't like me. I just knew. I knew she didn't. We butted heads. I knew in my gut.

Laura recalled that growing up, she found herself naturally falling into the roles she felt she fit best into, initially feeling as though she was "the worst child in the world." When her older sister, "the perfect child," got pregnant at nineteen, disappointing her parents, Laura jumped at the chance to replace her.

So again, it was a role that needed to be filled, so I took that. I'll be the good girl. I'll do everything right. I will do my homework, I will do my chores. So I jumped at that. I was good at creating situations, but at the same time, I remember having to jump into that role to be liked. And again, we talked about that later in life, my mom and I. The only way I thought I could get her to like me was to be the person I wasn't, but that wasn't the case. We talked at different times...and she was open enough and shared enough with me to open up her heart, and in a sense, she was my best friend.

Laura noted that while her tendency to go down a negative thought path could have damaged her relationship with her mother beyond repair, she credited a lot of time and many long conversations together in which they each discussed their perspectives with helping to heal their relationship, becoming best friends later in Laura's life.

We talked about that. So that's important. Just because you get a little blip like that, don't elaborate on it yourself. You have to discuss it with the person. Because you are going to go in the wrong direction with that little snippet of information.

While Laura's father is still alive, her mother had since passed away.

I know that she's in heaven. She is not in any pain. As close as my mom and I were, I didn't cry when she died. She was ready. She is where she is supposed to be. And I know I am probably different than most people; part of me thinks I'm a little weird, but people are supposed to die. And you can't hang on to them. You can't hang on to the physical part. You can hang on to their essence. I continue to talk to my mom all the time, and I have as much of a relationship with my mom years after she's passed as I did before.

Laura noted that over the years, through their open conversations, she learned to put herself in her mother's shoes, relating to her as a person.

You have to look at your parent. They are you. You have to give them allowances. You are going to make mistakes. I make mistakes. I've made mistakes as a parent. I wish I could take some things back. But you have to think that your kids are going to take what they need out of that. So you've got to look at your parent; put yourself in their shoes and what they are dealing with. My mom and I were transparent. Like I said, probably till I was 14, I did not like my mom. We butted heads. I wanted her to like me but she didn't, and I didn't like her. It wasn't until I was like 16 that we started changing, transitioned, and even then it took a little bit of time. But by the time I was in my early 30s, we were like best friends. But it was still a learning process. With your best friend you have to accept them for who they are and continue to talk. Find out why they do what they do and you do what you do and why you interact the way you do.

Despite personal struggles, her mother left a lasting impact on Laura's outlook on life. The conversations she facilitated as an adult helped to alleviate any guilt or regrets between the mother and daughter.

My mom was a phenomenal person. She acted mostly on what she was being told. And I think that it wasn't 'til she was in her 50s that she started to do what she thought was right for her. It wasn't until her 50s that she started listening to her own gut. And I think as generation to generation we want to give to the next generation a stepping stone up from where you went, and I think that's what she did to me. And even with the learning disability, she was going to make sure that wasn't something that could hold me back. She just gave me a platform to go upward.

While Laura's mother fought for her own children to have any future they could envision, she still had her own dreams for herself. Although Laura noted that music wasn't a staple in her house growing up, she recalled her mother's wishes for the afterlife that indicate her penchant for music after all.

My mom often said that when she goes to heaven, she is going to have long, thick, black hair and she's going to sing. She always felt that she didn't have a good singing voice, and she always wanted one. I hope she doesn't have long, thick, black hair because I wouldn't recognize her up there. But I know she's singing up there…I love my mom. She's my superstar.

Laura and her mother, Nancy, on Laura's wedding day

Conclusion

Motherhood is so much simpler when
you stop explaining yourself and just do
what works for you and your family.

—Proud Happy Mama

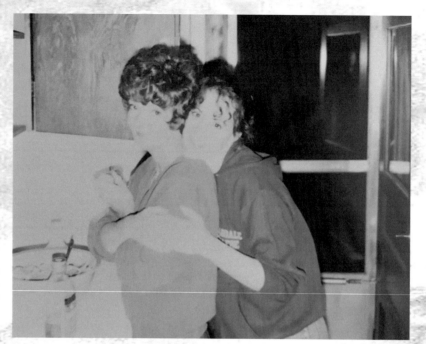

Upper left: Lisa Rigato with her mother, Theresa Rigato. *Lower:* Theresa Rigato.

Thank you for reading these stories and witnessing the great courage that has been shared whether from the mother or the child. We never know the impact we can have on one another and how our story may encourage someone struggling with life. We all have choices and can choose to hang onto the hurt from the past or to find something to be grateful for in the present. I choose gratitude for all the valuable lessons I learned from the loss of my family unit but the gain of my inner strength and respect for another's point of view.

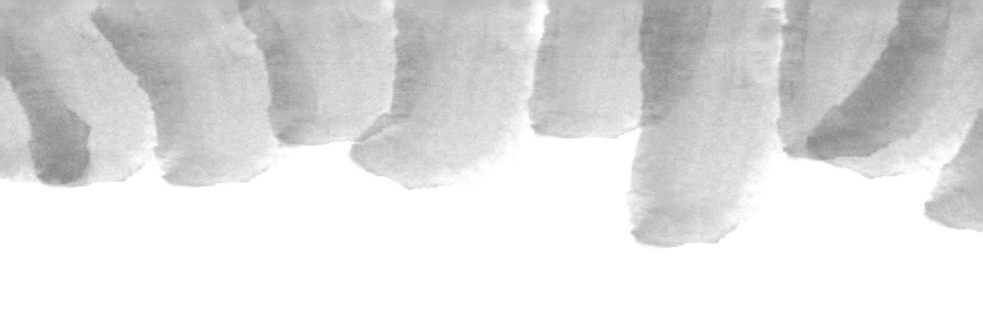

Children shouldn't have to sacrifice so that you can have the life you want. You make sacrifices so your children can have the life they deserve.

—Unknown

About the Author

Lisa Rigato was born in 1961 in a small suburb of Detroit but moved to the country to the even smaller town of Howell, Michigan, when she was eight years old with her parents and four siblings. Little did she know then that the cute boy that became her brother's first new friend would be the man she would come to marry thirty-four years later.

Lisa learned to appreciate the freedom that comes from using her imagination as the greatest form of entertainment as she embraced the differences between living in the suburb of a major city to the country where your closest neighbor could be a mile down that dirt road. It became a challenge and a weekly experience to be charged by *Mr. French*, the neighbors' bull, when taking the short cut across the pasture to go play with her friends.

When Lisa was a child, her parents purchased a property in Northern Michigan, and their summers were spent traversing the hundreds of acres of woods that surrounded the family cabin. It was there that she learned her affinity for finding the treasures of the earth—from sticks and feathers to leaves and rocks. Rockhounding around the Great Lakes has become her lifelong hobby. Unable to have children of her own, Lisa is passing on her love of rockhounding to her forty-plus nieces and nephews. They are her greatest joy and the primary inspiration for writing *Tell Me About Your Mother*.